COMMUNITY HELPERS

Judges

by Kieran Downs

BLASTOFF! READERS

BELLWETHER MEDIA • MINNEAPOLIS, MN

Blastoff! Readers are carefully developed by literacy experts to build reading stamina and move students toward fluency by combining standards-based content with developmentally appropriate text.

Level 1 provides the most support through repetition of high-frequency words, light text, predictable sentence patterns, and strong visual support.

Level 2 offers early readers a bit more challenge through varied sentences, increased text load, and text-supportive special features.

Level 3 advances early-fluent readers toward fluency through increased text load, less reliance on photos, advancing concepts, longer sentences, and more complex special features.

★ **Blastoff! Universe**

Reading Level

Grade **K**

Grades **1–3**

Grade **4**

This edition first published in 2021 by Bellwether Media, Inc.

No part of this publication may be reproduced in whole or in part without written permission of the publisher. For information regarding permission, write to Bellwether Media, Inc., Attention: Permissions Department, 6012 Blue Circle Drive, Minnetonka, MN 55343.

Library of Congress Cataloging-in-Publication Data

Names: Downs, Kieran, author.
Title: Judges / Kieran Downs.
Description: Minneapolis, MN : Bellwether Media, Inc. 2021. | Series: Blastoff! readers: Community helpers | Includes bibliographical references and index. | Audience: Ages 5-8 | Audience: Grades K-1 | Summary: "Developed by literacy experts for students in kindergarten through grade three, this book introduces judges to young readers through leveled text and related photos"–Provided by publisher"
Identifiers: LCCN 2019053754 (print) | LCCN 2019053755 (ebook) | ISBN 9781644871942 (library binding) | ISBN 9781681038186 (paperback) | ISBN 9781618919526 (ebook)
Subjects: LCSH: Judges–United States–Juvenile literature.
Classification: LCC KF8775 .D69 2021 (print) | LCC KF8775 (ebook) | DDC 347.73/14-dc23
LC record available at https://lccn.loc.gov/2019053754
LC ebook record available at https://lccn.loc.gov/2019053755

Editor: Betsy Rathburn   Designer: Laura Sowers

Printed in the United States of America, North Mankato, MN.

Table of Contents

Order in the Court!

Two people stand
before a judge.
They begin to **argue**.

The judge bangs
his **gavel**.
Order in the **court**!

gavel

What Are Judges?

Judges listen to court **cases**. They make sure cases are fair.

Judges work
for governments.
They explain laws.
They **settle** cases.

Judges work
in courtrooms.
They wear robes.
They sit at the bench.

Judge Gear

robes

gavel

bench

books

robe

bench

What Do Judges Do?

Judges make sure everyone in court follows the rules. They listen to facts.

Judges study the law. They look at past cases. This helps them make **rulings**.

What Makes a Good Judge?

Judges are good listeners. Fair judges listen to everyone equally.

Judge Skills

✓ fair   ✓ good reader

✓ smart   ✓ good listener

Judges are
good readers.
They study a lot
to know the law!

Glossary

argue

to disagree using words

gavel

a small tool that looks like a hammer; a gavel is used to call for order.

cases

things that are decided in a court of law

rulings

decisions made by judges

court

a place where questions about the law are answered

settle

to arrange an agreement between two or more sides

To Learn More

AT THE LIBRARY

Leaf, Christina. *Police Officers*. Minneapolis, Minn.: Bellwether Media, 2018.

Meltzer, Brad. *I am Sonia Sotomayor*. New York, N.Y.: Dial Books for Young Readers, 2018.

Schuh, Mari. *The Supreme Court*. Minneapolis, Minn.: Bellwether Media, 2021.

ON THE WEB

FACTSURFER

Factsurfer.com gives you a safe, fun way to find more information.

1. Go to www.factsurfer.com.

2. Enter "judges" into the search box and click 🔍.

3. Select your book cover to see a list of related content.

Index

The images in this book are reproduced through the courtesy of: FangXiaNuo, front cover; RichLegg, pp. 4-5, 6-7; sirtravelalot, pp. 8-9, 13 (bench); dcdebs, pp. 10-11; ESB Professional, pp. 12-13; Vectorpocket, p. 13 (robes); StudioSmart, p. 13 (gavel); studiovin, p. 13 (books); Gregg Vignal/ Alamy, pp. 14-15; Alina555, pp. 16-17; Image Source, pp. 18-19; Minerva Studio, pp. 20-21; fizkes, p. 22 (top left); Billion Photos, p. 22 (top right); ZozerEblola, p. 22 (middle left); MR.Yanukit, p. 22 (middle right); Nirat.pix, p. 22 (bottom left); Dragon Images, p. 22 (bottom right).